"Hello! Helpline!"

Parenting & Personal Strategies from a Hotline Professional

Nancy Burk

"Hello! Helpline!"

©2014 by Nancy Burk

New Jersey, United States of America

ISBN: 978-0-9886228-0-7

First edition

Cover design by Gina Mancini

Editorial by Word Metro
Publishing production by Word Metro Press

Additional editors: Megan Sullivan, Deborah Bossio, John Michael Burk and Susan Keats Taber

TABLE OF CONTENTS

ACKNOWLEDGEMENTS

Just as it takes a village to raise a child, the love and support of friends, family and coworkers have empowered me:

I thank my Crisis Hotline Family. The office staff, in particular, Laurie, Trish and Kathy, were supportive and contributed to both my having the courage to write this book and the opportunity to hone my philosophies.

I thank my parents, Jeanette and Hyman, and appreciate their love and that they did everything in their power to help me.

I thank my husband, Michael, for being supportive and appreciating my parenting skills.

I thank my friends, Debby, Sue and Cyndi, for their encouragement, everlasting friendship and love.

My immense gratitude to Joanne K. Halscheid for her wisdom in helping so many parents raise their children.

DEDICATION

I dedicate this book to my precious
children, Abagale and John Michael, who
are the reasons I am who I am today. Their
appreciation, love and support
are unparalleled.

INTRODUCTION

One purpose of this book is to tell you there is no one way to raise your child. There is no silver bullet strategy that can vanquish all conflict and no panacea that can solve all problems and guarantee success. This book is meant to prod you to take action to change and try something different. Don't *do more of the same that didn't work to begin with*. Make no mistake, finding your road is not always easy; it's not something you can accomplish in an afternoon. However, in one afternoon you might find an idea that leads to an "ah ha" moment that *springboards* you into finding another tool for your parenting arsenal. It's a process. It will involve some trial and error, reflective thought, and work. Most of all, it will require a willingness to try new things, to make mistakes, and to learn and grow as a person and as a parent.

I worked on a hotline, where people can call anonymously. In this book, I will refer to the hotline as the "Family Crisis Hotline" or "Crisis Hotline" to maintain the anonymity of both the hotline and its callers. On the Family Crisis Hotline I was not permitted to give advice. My job was to listen, reflect, brainstorm and give out resources from a large binder. We could only state facts. Along the way I developed my own general truths that I offered to help callers find direction.

Through my work on the hotline, my struggles and challenges of raising my own children, and listening to friends tell their stories, I have honed my philosophies on parenting, relationships and mindset. I have clawed and fought to find my road which is still evolving. I have always thought of my wants, desires and objectives as a destination and ideas, perspective and information as my way of getting there: my road! I hope that everyone finds their road because that is the beginning of finding your answers to life, relationships and parenting. Once you are set on a new plan, you must implement it. No one can discover answers and fix problem behaviors for you. You have to change yourself in order to elicit change in others.

I got to this point in my life by attending to bits of logic and skills proposed by others. I took to heart those things that rang true to me and then worked hard to incorporate them into my own behaviors. If a skill, mantra or philosophy I heard or read about sounded like something worthwhile and doable, then I used it as a springboard to postulate my own doctrine of parenting and life. I hope you can use some of my anecdotes, stories and philosophies as a springboard to find your own road.

Over time I realized that many of my ideas and philosophies overlapped. Just as there are literally two sides to a coin – heads and tails – many of the ideas I will explain combine or become integrated with one another. Often I use an integral part of one idea or concept to explain another. Many of these ideas or sayings I call mantras are italicized throughout the book and listed at the end.

Over the years, it has been my pleasure to speak with the callers on the hotline and to hear their stories, most of which were so heart-warming! Most people seemed to be desperate, eager, loving, willing to change and hard working. I could always hear the callers' despair, yet I could sense their deep love and commitment to trying to find help and answers for their families.

To me, talking and working with callers on the hotline has been a tribute to the will of the human spirit. To my pleasant surprise, people were often eager to accept the notion of changing their own behaviors. I don't know the names of the callers due to the all-important *anonymous* part of my work, but I do vividly remember many of their stories. All the names in these stories have been made up.

ABOUT THE AUTHOR

On a personal note, I've been married for over twenty-five years and I am the mother of two wonderful children. My daughter is twenty-five years old and my son is twenty-two. While they are not perfect, they are both smart, funny, independent and shining lights in the world. I am immensely proud of them both!

I attended Trenton State College (now called The College of New Jersey), where I earned a Bachelor's of Arts in Psychology and minored in business. I also have a Certification in Elementary Education, as well as a teaching Certification in Secondary Education to teach psychology. I then attended Rider University where I earned a Master's of Arts Degree in Counseling which afforded me my licensure as an Eligible Licensed Professional Counselor. I have worked for a family crisis hotline as a hotline professional for over fifteen years.

1

YOU CAN'T CHANGE OTHER PEOPLE; YOU CAN ONLY CHANGE YOURSELF

You can't change your mother, father, sister, brother, husband, wife, neighbor, dog or child! You can't change other people. You can only change yourself. Therefore, when facing a problem with your children or anybody else you need to ask yourself, "What can I do differently?" Parents want their children to change their behavior, but can you want and expect someone else to change, without even thinking about or attempting to change yourself? If I concentrate on trying to change someone else and put so much energy into feeling bad and trying to change someone else, I will be frustrated. So the correct avenue for your energy is to ask yourself, "Is there a behavior of mine that I can change, because this is the only thing I can do?"

There are often several behavioral changes we can make that will elicit different responses from others. For example, I can state what I need instead of wagging my finger at and complaining about my children's undesirable behavior. I talk more about this throughout the book.

Also, I can use a calm voice because it's not always what you say that is important, but how you say it. By changing one's voice, tone or affect, one can change the meaning of what is said. The same words in a different voice may be better received. If your boss at work yells at you to do something, you might tell him where to stick that job; whereas if your manager asks you kindly and politely, then you will probably be more eager to please him. Although you can't change other people, you can change something about how you react to or act with others. Consequently, your new behaviors will result in different responses. Remember, by eliciting the cooperation of others, one can get one's own needs met. This is a premise for the rest of my ideas.

2
A GOOD PARENT IS A GOOD TEACHER AND A GOOD MANAGER

Often parents think, "I don't ask my children to do things like going to school or helping in the house. I tell them. I am the parent. I am the authority and the boss. I'm not going to beg my child."

I try to explain on the hotline that companies spend millions of dollars on management training. Good managers elicit cooperation from their employees. Even though adults get paid to do a job, they are supervised in the workplace. Why is an adult in need of supervision in the workplace, especially when one is being paid to do this job? This bears repeating. An adult works and gets paid to do a job and has a supervisor or manager. Yet in our homes, with our own children whom we love, we often resent having to manage our children or set up a system for a positive outcome. We think we would be wimpy if we coax our children. Parents often believe they should just give their kids a direction one time or even better yet, the child should just know to do certain behaviors. We often act like our children are an inconvenience and our subjects to boss around. I believe this thought system is simply misguided. If workers who get paid to do a job need good management and supervision, then it seems perfectly reasonable that our own beloved children may need and benefit from the same. Why shouldn't our own children receive the advantage at home that strangers get in the workplace? The best managers elicit cooperation and devotion from their employees. An effective manager doesn't sit 'on high' barking orders or yelling at their employees. Remember, *a good parent is a good teacher and a good manager.*

So what I suggest is that you be a good manager in your home. For instance, some parents impart arbitrary curfews on their children. My question to you is why 9:00? Why not 9:15 or 9:05 or 8:54? I say let's make sense of the curfew issue. You might explain, "Well sweetie, I have to get up for work so 9:00 is the latest I can stay awake. On the weekends, of course, bedtime and curfew is later because we both can stay up later. Also, if you're having a good time, then call and let me know so I don't worry and we can work out an extension." Remember, a good parent is a good teacher. You're trying to teach empathy by showing the reasoning behind the curfew. By arbitrarily declaring a curfew and acting like a king or queen over your subjects, you might experience an uprising to overthrow the throne.

Often what you need from your children is valid. So instead of demonstrating random behaviors and making arbitrary demands, elicit your child's cooperation to your reasonable and valid end.

3

EXERCISE FOR CHANGE

Here is an exercise. Stand up, walk over to a wall, place both of your hands on the wall and start pushing. Pretend you are pushing against my hands. Continue expending energy pushing until you realize that you can't move the wall. You realize you can't change the wall or me. You can stop pushing when you realize you can't change others; you can only change yourself. Now you stop pushing. Notice the wall stopped pushing you. Think of some other behaviors you can adopt that may be more effective in getting your needs met, instead of pushing.

4
EMOTIONS, BEHAVIORS AND THOUGHTS

As humans we have three parts of ourselves that we can change. We have our emotions, our behaviors and our thoughts. If one changes any of these parts of themselves, then the other parts will change.

There is a saying, "Turn your frown upside down." When we smile, we actually feel a happy sensation. By changing something physical, our emotions will change and we feel a little better. For instance, do you remember a time when you were sad or angry and someone cracked a joke that made you laugh? You felt better and perhaps you were able to calm down and think through your problem. Thus, changing a physical behavior will change our emotions and thoughts.

Another mode of operation is to rely on one's thoughts to change one's emotions and behaviors. For instance, let's talk about the parent who is so mad and fed up with their child's very messy room. On the hotline many parents complain that their child is lazy and spoiled from all the electronics he or she is given. This labeling a child as "lazy" and "spoiled" in turn causes the parent to become enraged at their child. If one perceives their kid in a negative light, then one will react negatively. If one's thoughts are negative, then one's words and actions will coincide with this and the parent may yell, scold and punish. However, if the parent labels the child who hasn't cleaned his room as normal, although not pleasant, the parent will react differently. If the parent can change his thoughts and labeling of the child or situation, then the parent will feel differently and consequently behave differently. Perhaps, one resigns herself to the notion that rooms of teenagers are messy and this is normal. Perhaps, the parent can realize my child is a good student, funny, loves soccer and her room is messy often. Now instead of yelling, the parent can work at eliciting their child's cooperation. He or she can speak calmly and explain, "I really need our home to be clean. We have to vacuum in your room once a week to keep our home clean of bugs and lint." The more you practice perceiving your child in a realistic and positive light, the more your emotions will follow suit. Perhaps, you will feel calmer, happier and more hopeful. Our behavior, our emotions and our thoughts are all related and affected by each other.

My friend Sonia's ten-year-old son, Harrison, seemed to get angry quickly. One day he started to raise his voice to his mom, but instantaneously realized that his father was in the family room. Sonia exclaimed, "You were going to yell at me before you saw Dad sitting there!" to which the father without moving a muscle said in a gruff voice, "You treat your mother the same whether I'm here or not!" A few days later Sonia sat with Harrison and spoke to him about his anger. She candidly explained, "Anger is a normal emotion. We can't help how we feel, but you're not allowed to direct your anger toward me." They spoke for a while and then Sonia brainstormed with Harrison. She suggested, "The next time you're angry, how about hitting the pillows on the couch. You can't hit the frame. You're not allowed to hurt yourself." They even practiced hitting the pillows and yelling. She further even practiced with him taking a deep breath when he was finished to let the anger go because, she explained to Harrison, "Anger can build on itself."

A few days later Sonia heard a racket in the living room and yelled, "What are you doing?" To which Harrison shouted back, "You told me I could hit the pillows!" So even though the noise sounded disre-spectful, Sonia was quiet until the ruckus stopped and her son was sitting quietly. Then she joined him in the living room. She asked him how it felt, to which he just shrugged. Kids often don't know or can't articulate how they feel. Then Sonia turned the situation into a positive and told her son enthusiastically, "You did a good job. You remembered what we practiced and did it. You're a good boy!"

The point here is that Sonia's thought that anger is a normal emotion led her to behave and think like an adult – the parent. Consequently, she had brainstormed to find an acceptable outlet for her son's emotions and then turned the acceptable display of anger into a positive. Kudos!!! Her goal was to help her son solve a problem. If Sonia had gotten mad and punished or yelled, perhaps things might have escalated. It is clear that Sonia's success with her son was due to anti-inflammatory thoughts, her brainstorming and her ability to follow through.

5
MORE LABELING

While there are different parts of us that we can change, mislabeling behaviors was a common issue on the hotline. Labeling behaviors negatively seems to be our default setting. It seems that it is not in our repertoires to automatically label behaviors in a positive light. Similarly, we tend to pigeon-hole the motivations of behaviors in the face of a problem or a crisis. For instance, on the hotline, if a child was angry or acting out, then the mother blamed this behavior on her pending divorce. Meanwhile, another caller blamed her child's non-compliance on the child's diagnosis of Attention Deficit Disorder.

Yet another friend was going through a divorce and wanted her college-aged son to go to a counselor, but he refused. It was clear to me that her son was not that upset about the divorce. She obviously was! While counseling is a great idea for anyone, especially through a crisis or life change, we have to be careful not to assume our children feel the way we expect them to or the same way we feel. There are many variables that can contribute to your child's behavior. I just want you to be careful not to jump to conclusions because then you have cornered yourself and can only react to the labels you have set in your mind.

Another example of labeling shows in this priceless article my friend showed me. It paints a picture of the havoc of negative labeling in one's own mind.

Thoughts On Failure

John Pierpont died a failure. In 1866, at age eighty-one, he came to the end of his days as a government clerk in Washington, D.C., with a long string of personal defeats abrading his spirit.

Things began well enough. He graduated from Yale, which his grandfather had helped found, and chose education as his profession with some enthusiasm.

He was a failure at school teaching. He was too easy on his students. And so he turned to the legal world for training.

He was a failure as a lawyer. He was too generous to his clients and too concerned about justice to take the cases that brought good fees. The next career he took up was that of dry-goods merchant.

He was a failure as a businessman. He could not charge enough for his goods to make a profit and was too liberal with credit.

In the meantime, he had been writing poetry, and though it was published, he didn't collect enough royalties to make a living.

He was a failure as a poet. And so he decided to become a minister, went off to Harvard Divinity School, and was ordained as minister of the Hollis Street Church in Boston. But his position for Prohibition and against slavery got him crosswise with the influential members of his congregation, and he was forced to resign.

He was a failure as a minister. Politics seemed a place where he could make some difference, and he was nominated as the Abolition party candidate for governor of Massachusetts. He lost. Undaunted, he ran for Congress under the banner of the Free Soil party. He lost.

He was a failure as a politician. The Civil War came along, and he volunteered as a chaplain of the 22nd Regiment of the Massachusetts Volunteers. Two weeks later, he quit, having found the task too much of a strain on his health. He was seventy-six years old. He couldn't even make it as a chaplain.

Someone found him an obscure job in the back offices of the Treasury Department in Washington, and he finished out the last five years of his life as a menial file clerk. He wasn't very good at that, either. His heart was not in it.

John Pierpont died a failure. He had accomplished nothing he set out to do or be. There is a small memorial stone marking his grave in Mount Auburn Cemetery in Cambridge, Massachusetts. The words in the granite read: POET, PREACHER, PHILOSOPHER, PHILANTHROPIST.

From this distance in time, one might insist that he was not, in fact, a failure. His commitments to social justice, his desire to be a loving human being, his active engagement in the great social issues of his times, and his faith in the power of the human mind — these are not failures. And much of what he thought of as defeat became success. Education was reformed, legal processes were improved, credit laws were changed, and, above all, slavery was abolished once and for all.

Why am I telling you this? ...... In one very important sense, John Pierpont was not a failure. Every year we carry in our hearts and minds a memorial to him. Every year around December we hear it, so we think of it as a

Christmas carol, but it really has nothing to do with Christmas. It's a simple song about the simple joy of whizzing through the cold dark night of winter's gloom in a sleigh pulled by one horse, with a company of friends, laughing and singing. No more. No less. "Jingle Bells."

John Pierpont wrote "Jingle Bells."

To write a song that stands for the simplest joys, to write a song that three or four hundred million people around the world know — a song about something none of them have ever done but can imagine — a song that every one of us, large and small, can hoot out the moment the chord is struck on the piano and the chord is struck in our spirit — well, that's not failure.

John Pierpont never knew the impact he made on the world. His name is largely forgotten. But his words live on. So this December, when you hear "Jingle Bells," and you will most assuredly hear it, I want you to think of John Pierpont, the failure.

Fondly,

Kaye (Fulghum, p 14-18, Kaye, n.p.)

Be careful how you label your children's behaviors. It's easy to be negative. Place your energy into trying to be positive. Turn your negative thoughts to positive thoughts. Try to remember, *don't be negative and nasty, be positive and pleasant.*

For example, when your child doesn't want to continue playing soccer, instead of thinking and maybe telling him he is lazy or fickle, turn your thoughts to a positive. How about, *maybe this child is ready for a change* or *my child needs to find something else that may interest him* or *I'm proud of him for trying new things.* People can live their whole lives feeling bad about themselves. Belittling oneself is not acceptable. Likewise, belittling your children is unacceptable. As parents, it is your job to teach your children to see, acknowledge and appreciate any and all of their accomplishments. Children learn this from watching and listening to their parents. Any situation becomes a teachable moment.

A teachable moment is any time that you can turn a situation into a time to teach something to your child. Children learn to be positive from watching and listening to their parents putting a positive spin on any scenario.

When I visit the local mall, I frequently see mothers scolding their children over bad behavior. I often butt in and say to the mother sweetly, "Awww, he's a good boy! You know I look at the situation from the little boy's point of view. You and I can shop in the mall all day. But if we went to a car shop like Pep Boys, we would both probably start yawning and become fidgety in about two minutes! Right?! (Then we laugh together.) Well that's probably how he feels in this mall. I bet he could shop for a long time in Toys"R"Us. It's hard when you want to concentrate on shopping, but maybe you can sing with him. He's a good boy."

Every time I interject this other view of one's child's behavior, the mother seems to change her demeanor. Perhaps, just a heightened awareness helps. Shopping moms have to be careful about labeling their little boy or girl as impatient or bad because he or she is asking questions or singing a song or even whining. In fact, to me these little boys and girls are amazing because they are often inter-acting, being polite and entertaining themselves. We need to remember that shopping is boring for children! So in this example, when shopping with children, mothers need to be careful when labeling the situation.

Years ago, a darling, young woman called so upset over her son not listening. When I asked her some basic questions like, "What didn't he do?" or "How old is your son?" she revealed that her son didn't brush his teeth and he was four years old! Oh my goodness! I started to laugh and encouraged her to see that this was perfectly normal. No little kid voluntarily brushes his teeth or washes or cleans up! What was she thinking? The essence of this example is to show how all of us can get bogged down in our expectation and disappointment. I impressed upon her that if she wished to instill good habits in her son, she could find ways to make a game of it and to motivate and praise him. Years ago my friend's mother would leave M&M candies on the bathroom counter so that he would run to find them and eat them. Then she would sit with him as he brushed the chocolate out of his teeth. Finally, they would admire his clean teeth in the mirror.

The moral is to be careful of your expectations in any situation. I still remember this scared young mother and hope she is labeling her son's behaviors in a realistic and positive light so she can feel better and function more effectively.

6
PERFECT

When my friend Mary's little girl was two years old, Mary was beside herself thinking her little blonde-haired angel was an evil devil child. This little girl never seemed to care about hurting anybody else's feelings. After many conversations with Mary, I realized that my friend was lonely, bored and distraught like many stay-at-home moms. Mary wrote this passage about her toddler:

I don't think I'm going to get through the terrible two's. My little girl is so contrary and obstinate to the extent that she often won't hug her father or me or her grandparents. And it seems that she never shows affection toward her father unless he has a goody for her – kind of like a trained porpoise, but colder. Yes, my little girl, Annabel, tries my patience to put it mildly. I took a deep breath, let it out along with some of my tension and decided to take the day in sections. The morning is for Sesame Street *and getting dressed. The midmorning is for lunch and play. The afternoon is for a two-hour nap – thank heavens!*

The late afternoon is Sesame Street *again and early evening is dinner. And night time is the savior because I know the day is almost over and she will be asleep by 10:00. Yes, she doesn't get to sleep until 10:00! Now it is important to note at this time that* Sesame Street *is not just a TV show, but a lifeline to sanity. You see when Annabel is preoccupied with this educational program, I am temporarily relieved of fetching cups of apple juice, pretzels, reading little books, dressing and redressing (she loves to get naked), changing diapers, and dealing with her moods. There is no telling when you will rub her the wrong way. Anything can set her off. And this morning was no exception. I mustered up some courage and enthusiastically said, "Annabel, let's go to Burger King for lunch." Burger King is a kid's paradise with burgers, chicken, french fries, soda and a play area/jungle gym! She promptly replied, "No, I don't wanna go to Buga King!" I baited her by saying, "I'm going to Burger King." She whined, "I wanna go to Buga King." I sat on the edge of my bed and wept for a few moments and wondered if I would see a bit of remorse, sympathy or love from this round little face staring at me. She looked bewildered, but not concerned that I was sad. So I took another deep breath and conjured up some more energy. I dressed her in an adorable outfit and managed to coax her into letting me put her hair in pigtails, all to make her look cute and appealing to me so I might like her better.*

After reading what Mary wrote, I felt so sorry for my friend. It's not easy being a caretaker, not to mention a stay-at-home mom. Mary had ended up calling a hotline. She told me about the call and said that although the hotline worker had sounded sleepy in the middle of the day, she said something so profound to Mary. After Mary complained about her toddler for a few minutes, the hotline worker said, "Don't expect your child to be perfect or you will be disappointed." My friend used this as her springboard and mantra to maintain realistic expectations from then on. *It is normal for a toddler to be contrary,* she realized. In retrospect, she was frustrated by her inability to label her daughter's behaviors correctly. After her realization, Mary continued to gently teach her child right from wrong and how to socialize. She emphasized her family values and took her responsibilities of parenting to heart. Once Mary maintained a more realistic attitude, over time she worried less often and she wasn't so sad.

Mary revealed to me that she realizes when she was a young, stay-at-home mother, she felt isolated and didn't see the whole picture nor label her baby's behaviors correctly. She labeled her daughter's behaviors negatively and therefore was disappointed and sad a lot. Now, her precious daughter is a gift to her every day and she is very clear about that.

Presently, Mary's little girl, Annabel, is in her twenties. She is hysterically funny, so smart and quick witted, beautiful, supportive, empathetic and validating to her mother.

7
KIDS ON A PLAYGROUND

Often parents seem so angry with their children. This is understandable and you are entitled to feel angry. You can feel any way you want. However, you do not have carte blanche to act any way you want. Often parents behave like *kids on the playground*. When parents engage in a screaming match or name calling, it reminds me of kids on a playground exchanging *tit for tat*. For example, in retaliation for a child not completing his chores, one parent on the hotline kept digging, "Well, you're a brat!" or "You're lazy." Name calling is never an appropriate behavior for a parent, nor is it effective.

Another example of parents misbehaving is when they try to hurt their kid in the meanest way they can think of on the spot. Many parents threaten to take TV, phones and other things away as a punishment, hoping to motivate their children to do their chores and schoolwork. However, time and time again I hear parents try this tactic to no avail. Taking things away just to spite your child does not work.

In another example, one parent scolded because her child had not completed chores, "Now I'm not going to bother making your lunch. You'll just have to buy lunch and if you're hungry, then that's too bad. And if you're hungry when you get home, you won't get a snack. I'm not going to make you anything to eat." This mother sounded just like a little kid at recess.

Trying to get even by name calling, taking stuff away or threatening in anger doesn't work. What is important are your parenting strategies. You will have better results more often if you base what you say and do on what's relevant to the situation. Natural consequences are better than arbitrary punishments. Instead of this mother lashing out with threats, how about a maturely executed natural consequence like, "Since these chores weren't done, I will have to do them. So I'm sorry, but I won't have the time to make your lunch. You'll buy lunch today." One is calm and firm – not vindictive. Now this will work if your child likes taking his lunch and not buying lunch. Otherwise, the consequence has to be changed to something that motivates your child. The point here is don't lash out. Don't be a kid on the playground. Think!

In another example, I have noticed the all-important cleaning of rooms is so prevalent and yields much distress for parents. I believe it is important to be clear about your reasons for why one should keep a room clean. Not attracting ants, preserving the furniture, providing unencumbered space for others to enjoy and making our common space welcoming for guests seem like good reasons. If your reasons are significant and compelling, you're more likely to find that your child will find them significant and compelling too. However, their own bedrooms may become a war zone anyway. Beware to pick your battles carefully. Whatever you do, remember, you are the adult – not a kid on the playground.

Recently, in another example, a lovely woman I will call Laura was dealing with her stepson, Greg's volatile behaviors. She said he was diagnosed with both anxiety disorder and bipolar disorder. He destroyed property and hit family members, which is unacceptable. You and your family are entitled to be safe in your home. My heart went out to her and I felt so badly for her. Laura said she was exhausted and, indeed, she sounded overwhelmed and fed up. She intended to use the resources I gave her to contact some doctors and programs for her stepson and family. However, I had the sense that she could still tweak some of her own behaviors. For instance, when her stepson yelled that his curtains needed to be hemmed, she replied to him angrily, "Do it yourself," because he didn't say it nicely. She admitted that this was not working. So perhaps it would be more effective if she said in a solicitous manner,

"Could you please sew my curtains? I need them hemmed." Then ask him to repeat this. With both parents encouraging him to restate what he wants, in a polite voice, it might become routine. Restating his request politely lends him to getting more used to behaving politely through repetition. We all learn through repetition. Some children need more repetitive training than others. That is, some need the experience of saying or doing something over and over again correctly to really *get it*. Unfortunately, parents need an exorbitant amount of patience to do this. I wish I had a patience pill. I would be the richest person in the world!

It's been my experience that being patient and behaving like the teacher we want to be is hard to do when our children push our buttons, ruffle our feathers and ultimately hurt our feelings. Sometimes the behaviors that work are counterintuitive. One can be firm, yet calm and show empathy in one's voice. Moreover, *necessity is the mother of invention.* When your current behaviors don't work, then search and try something else until you stumble upon what does work.

8
BRAINSTORMING FOR SOLUTIONS

Anna, my friend, had a son named Jacob and when he was six years old and in first grade, there was a little problem that I have often talked about on the hotline. Jacob was a bright little boy who loved animals but didn't particularly like going to school and complained about it on occasion. He never put up a fuss or made a scene when going to school, but he did complain about not liking school.

One day after a back-to-school night, his teacher explained that Jacob never finished his morning assignment like the other kids. So she had been keeping him in for recess as a consequence just like she would have done with any of the other kids. When Jacob came home the next day, Anna and her husband asked him why he hadn't finished the morning's writing assignment which was "Which would you rather be, a bird or a fish?" Jacob snidely retorted, "Well, I don't know which I would rather be and I could change my mind tomorrow..." Remember he was only six years old. With a sigh and a smile on her lips, Anna shook her head in the wake of her little boy's nonconformance and cockiness. She called the guidance counselor, Mrs. Joanne K. Halscheid, the next day. This wonderful guidance counselor suggested calling Jacob's teacher to elicit her cooperation to formulate another strategy to promote cooperation of Anna's son. After all, teachers often have private contracts with individual students. Halscheid acknowledged that what the teacher was doing repeatedly simply wasn't working. We often "do more of the same that didn't work to begin with" were Mrs. Halscheid's words (personal communication, 1998) that reverberate in Anna's mind to this day. The underlying message, in other words, is if something isn't working, then change it. So Anna called Jacob's teacher whom Anna liked very much and of whom she thought very highly. She was a great teacher and a charming person. Anna asked her if she had any individual contracts with pupils and if the teacher could alter the consequences for Jacob. Anna brainstormed new ideas with the teacher. Anna explained that she wanted Jacob to enjoy school more, so she wanted him to have recess. She asked the teacher if instead of finishing the morning assignment during recess, Anna would see to it that Jacob would do the assignment when he got home if he hadn't finished it for the morning assignment. Anna's brainstorm idea was well received by the teacher and as long as there was a consequence, then it seemed fair in accordance with the other students who completed their morning assignments. The teacher agreed to this individual contract and to the delight of Anna, Jacob never missed another morning assignment simply because he did not want to do it for homework! The lesson learned here is that one needs to brainstorm to find what works. I like this story of Jacob and his morning assignment because doing something different worked.

You wouldn't think, "Boy, my child is so bad and needy for needing braces." If one of your children needs braces, you don't put braces on your other children. Of course not! Some children need braces, some need allergy shots, some need more time alone, while others need tutoring. I often say, "Just give your children what they need and they are not bad for needing these things."

What is the best reward or consequence? For example, if someone places you in a maze and tells you there is a piece of cheese at the end but you are not hungry or do not like cheese, you probably are not going to work to find the cheese. However, for instance, if you place me in a maze and tell me there is a diamond ring at the end, I will be motivated to find my way out of the maze to retrieve my ring because I love jewelry!

When addressing what motivates your children, you are going to have to try different things. Remember, *necessity is the mother of invention*. That is, when you are beside yourself with despair over a behavior exhibited by your child, brainstorming and figuring out what you can do differently will eventually work. Quite often we find our way through trial and error. Just don't stop trying different things.

Another great example that often comes to mind is a story involving my friend, Melinda, and her daughter, Becca, who was about eight years of age. Becca was a very smart little girl who was a bit moody from time to time. Melinda would use the time-out method which gave consequences to the child for inappropriate behavior and gave Melinda precious time apart from her daughter to calm down. Melinda felt empowered after reading the book *123 Magic* by Thomas W. Phelan, Ph.D., which in very simple language teaches about "time-out." Melinda thought she was very clear in explaining exactly what behaviors she wanted from her daughter. She even role-played so Becca could actually see, hear and feel the tone and words that epitomized what being nicer and kinder in the home really meant. Melinda explained softly but seriously, "Our family is just like a society and you have to be polite and kind with us, just like you would with anyone else."

Little Becca would go to her room for eight minutes, but often come out still unhappy and miserable with everyone to her mother's dismay. So one day out of exasperation, Melinda just wanted to 'stick it' to Becca. Melinda ordered Becca to go to her room for time out. Except this time she told her to stay in her room until she was able to be pleasant and polite within the family. Becca went to her room and Melinda thought, *Ha, Ha, I got the better of her. I stuck it to her!* Well, some forty minutes later Becca was still in her room. Melinda called me so upset that Becca hadn't come out of her room yet and exclaimed, "That little girl is purposefully being stubborn and not coming out just to spite me!" A little while later Becca came out of her room happy and pleasant! Melinda was shocked! Little Becca had been playing in her room and forgot she was even in time-out. Melinda had mislabeled her daughter's behavior. Becca was not being spiteful to her mother. She was decompressing.

In retrospect, time was exactly what little Becca needed. She needed down time for herself. In fact, to this day as she sails through college, she needs her down time. It was by accident and desperation that Melinda found an answer and a piece of the puzzle with her funny and loving little girl. In the end by giving her daughter extra time by herself,

Melinda not only got a pleasant child, but she was also able to get her own needs met. And isn't that what consequences are really for? Getting your needs met? Eliciting behavioral changes from your children is what you're aiming for. So remember to try something different to elicit different behavior from others.

9
I NEED

On the hotline, one mother I'll call Linda sticks out in my mind. She was very narrowly focused on her daughter, Erika's cell phone use. I could not figure out why this cell phone bothered Linda so much. She wouldn't give me a straight answer. Linda just kept complaining about all the times her daughter was talking on her cell phone. Perhaps, Erika was staying up late talking on the phone and was having difficulty staying awake the next day at school. Or maybe, Linda felt hurt from a lack of attention from her daughter. Did Linda need more time and attention from her daughter? In any case, Linda found herself in battles with her daughter over whether or not she could use her cell phone and moreover, Linda was distraught over this cell phone issue.

Linda needed to focus on the behaviors she needed from her daughter, instead of her tunnel vision about the cell phone use. You need to manage instead of micro manage or you may find that neither you nor your child are getting your needs met. As Sylvester Stallone said as Rambo in *First Blood*, "I'll give you a war you won't believe." This may constitute the attitude you provoke from your child if you concentrate on the wrong thing.

State what you need. For instance, Linda may have planned a family meeting to ensure a calmer time period. Then Linda could have explained to Erika, "I need you to wake up in the morning of your own volition with your own alarm clock, get dressed and get to the bus on time every morning. I need you to be alert during the day. I don't want you to take naps because this messes up your sleep schedule. I also need you to be pleasant and polite – not moody." Linda then needs to explain behaviorally what *pleasant* means. Some role playing may help make the definition clear. Then Linda must tell her daughter, "I also need you to complete your homework." Then, "How do you feel about what I just said?" Erika may respond with an array of answers like, "Oh brother!" with an eye roll. Linda restates what she needs from her daughter. Linda continues this process until she gets from Erika, "Okay, Mom!"

A parent's job here is to get a commitment of a particular behavior from their child. When the child commits to a behavior, now you and your child are on the same side. Remember you can't change others. You can only elicit others' commitment to change their behaviors.

Next, Linda can ask Erika, "What might be a consequence of not waking up on time or getting to the bus stop on time or being grouchy?" Again the mother wants to get the child to agree to a preset consequence if these parameters are not met. Perhaps, a consequence of a set bedtime with all electronics turned off may be agreed upon if the child doesn't wake up on time or is sleepy during the day. Linda may suggest, "If you have trouble waking up in the morning, then it seems you need a better sleep routine." If your child is given a say in her consequence even though you might be the one to suggest some reasonable alternative behaviors, then the consequence won't be resented as much because it was not arbitrarily heaped upon the child without warning. At work you wouldn't want your boss telling you, "Stand up. Sit down. Stand up. Now sit down." It's annoying to have someone barking orders at us. So don't do that to your children.

In the end, the point is that this child can't stay up all night on the phone and simultaneously follow the rules to which she committed. I believe it's the parents' job to focus on what is needed from their child. They need to realize their bottom line. This mother on the hotline was so focused on being disgruntled about the time her daughter spent on her cell phone. She was seeing a situation through this severe tunnel vision. I kept wondering why she couldn't realize the problem was not about the phone. It was the lack of direction she was giving her daughter. Her mental road was quite muddled and when I was listening to her, I couldn't help but think that Erika would never be able to stay awake at night if she was waking up in the morning and being alert all day.

Now here is the hard part – following through! Linda would have to follow through with the consequences that they both set forth, but not in a nasty way, mind you. For example, the morning Erika can't wake up or misses the bus, Linda might illuminate, "Okay sweetie. It seems you were too tired this morning to wake up, so tonight bedtime is at 10:00 and all electronics are off like we agreed upon." One doesn't need to yell or be mean. Quite often simply following through with a consequence combined with a spoonful of sugar is the best teaching tool. If we yell a lot or are angry often, then children may learn to tune us out or learn to receive negative attention. In turn, we may get used to interacting by always pointing out the bad or harping on the mistakes and yelling about them. Mary Poppins sang it best. "Just a spoonful of sugar helps the medicine go down."

10
FINDING YOUR ROAD

You need to find *your* road. Whatever your problems, you must find your road, then you can go from there. *Finding your way* is what I call *finding your road*. Simply put, when looking for a sweater, you don't go to the grocery store or you'll be disappointed. That is, be clear about your destination and how you intend to get there.

For example a lot of divorced parents, both mothers and fathers who sound caring and good, worry about their ex-spouses being either too permissive or even abusive in their homes. A lovely woman whom I will call Norma called the hotline overwhelmed with her situation. She was in the middle of a divorce and her estranged husband was delinquent in child support payments. But the reason for calling was that she felt like an ineffective mother. She felt like she was always saying, "No, no, no." She was distraught and figured she was a bad mom. Once again the main issue revolved around her twelve-year-old daughter using her cell phone too much – particularly texting. Furthermore, the daughter, whom I will call Shana, was texting her father's girlfriend about problems with kids rebuffing her in school. Norma intercepted a text from this woman reportedly stating that she would beat up the other kids! I couldn't believe an adult would behave so poorly and say such a volatile thing. Really? She threatened violence?

So what could Norma do to both thwart violence and help her daughter find appropriate resources for help? Of course, I promoted going to school authorities in the wake of threats of violence in the school. Schools have "zero violence tolerance" policies now. Moreover, I wanted her to find a more positive road.

Empowering her daughter with other resources like private counselors or school counselors is one place to start. Also, if Shana was doting on what I call the "yna yna," which are the little things people do and say, the minutiae, then Shana needed to concentrate more on herself and less on others. Remember, Shana can't change other kids' behaviors. We all want to feel accepted and liked but, moreover, we all must find hobbies in life that make us happy and interest us. So, "How about encouraging her to develop her interests," I suggested. I explained that developing one's own interests and focusing on oneself develops self-esteem and direction and provides purpose. I told her a true story about someone I knew named Mary whose thirteen-year-old son was Ben.

Ben played baseball in the spring and fall. But his knee gave out and he needed surgery. Now with rehabilitation and healing, the high school team was not really attainable for him for a long time. So Mary elicited her son's cooperation by stating, "I need you to do something." He had to join an extracurricular activity. That is, she said, "it is incumbent upon me to make sure you develop your interests." After all, as his mother, it was her job to make sure Ben tried as many things as he could and learned to develop and continue to develop his interests. Ben angrily balked, "I don't want to join anything and be too busy every day like everybody else!" So Mary coaxed, "Well, I'll just look online at what extracurricular activities your school has. Okay?" She kept repeating this until he relented, shrugged and said, "Okay." Well, schools quite often have hundreds of activities, teams and clubs. So she started reading some of the teams and clubs that were listed. Now, what is unbeknown to you is that Ben would watch television while playing chess on an electronic chess board. So Mary suggested the chess club, which met three times per week, to which Ben responded to with an 'against the grain' attitude. He complained, "I don't want to go to a chess club." Ben's father was sitting there and piped up sarcastically with, "Oh, how terrible. You get to play chess for an hour three times per week. How terrible!" Mary continued to explain her position; she needed Ben to try something and get involved. I explained to the caller that Mary never wagged her finger at Ben nor reprimanded like, "You have to do this. I told you you're going to do this." Mary was calm and steadfast. Finally, Ben relented again and said, "Okay," he would join the chess team. He seemed to enjoy it and would come home relaying funny little stories about the kids on the chess team. Toward the end of the year Mary asked Ben, "Aren't you glad you joined the chess team?" To which Ben responded snippily, "No, I would rather be home! No, I don't like to be on a team!" The next year he joined the chess team again on his own. He continued to bring home and relay funny stories from chess club. This year when Mary asked him, "Aren't you glad you joined?" she was sure her son would smile and agree whole-heartedly. However, Ben abruptly retorted, "No, I would rather be home." In his junior year, Ben again joined the chess team of his own volition and showered the family once again with team stories. So sheepishly yet another time, Mary asked Ben, "Aren't you glad you joined the chess team?" This time with a smile Ben affirmed, "Yes." And to this day, even after graduation he continues his friendships with many of his chess teammates and is glad to have taken this road.

Norma, the mother who was distraught about being a bad mom and her estranged husband's poor influence, could use these skills to set her child on her own road. Instead of worrying about the other children's poor, mean or immature behaviors, this road of developing one's own interests and concentrating on improving one's self is clearly more productive.

11

DON'T PUT YOUR HEAD ON YOUR CHILD'S BODY; REFLECT

Often parents don't know how to help their children. I hear the love, frustration and desperation in the parents I speak to on the hotline. Often we try to help our children by giving them advice. But the problem is *you can't put your head on your child's body.* One man on the hotline advised his child, "I would just give those bullies a taste of their own medicine." This advice seems very inflammatory and could cause more trouble — maybe even a physical altercation, which would be unacceptable. More often, when a child is afraid to go to school, we tend to try to appease our children by saying, "There is nothing to be afraid of." If they say something is terrible and we say "no, don't worry about it" or "no, it's not scary or bad," then it seems like we are arguing, not validating and, moreover, not really hearing them. Sometimes our advice is not good or effective.

Believe it or not, reflecting is a much more effective response. Reflecting is when you repeat what your child is explaining and their feelings about it. So let's say your child says in despair, "I tripped on the way home and scraped my knee" with tears in her eyes. You can mirror back, "Awww, you scraped your knee and it's all bloody and it hurts!" Furthermore, you can state what you heard by saying "it sounds like …" or "I heard you say …" or "it seems like you …" You state what happened and how you perceive your child feels about it. For example, "It sounds like you're really upset about what happened in school today." Or "It seems like you are really proud of your accomplishment today!" You become just like a mirror that reflects an image. The mirror doesn't have an opinion. It just objectively shows you the truth of your appearance. We, as humans, then judge ourselves either in a positive or negative light as a result of an image in the mirror. Reflecting also allows you not to have to have all the answers all the time. The truth is that you probably won't have all the answers, or know what to say, or what advice to give your children. Often we feel helpless. Reflecting takes the pressure off of you. Really listening is a gift to our children. When our children feel heard, they know they have someone to go to who is on their side.

One example comes to mind when my friend's child just cried and didn't want to go to school for no apparent reason. My friend Jane's daughter, Hannah, whined, "I'm afraid!" Hannah was around six years old and in first grade. Jane tried to reason with her daughter and cajoled, "There's nothing to be afraid of." However, nothing seemed to soothe little Hannah. One morning after Hannah was crying and Jane pushed her on the bus, Jane was shaking. She felt so bad and was sick to her stomach. Her poor baby!

She just wanted to protect her Hannah and make everything better. So on this day Jane called the guidance counselor, Mrs. Halscheid (personal communication 1996), who directed Jane to stop trying to fix things. Halscheid asked, "If you could change this situation, would you have changed it already?" To which Jane answered, "Of course I would have." Halscheid responded, "So stop trying to fix it." She explained, "Every time you tell Hannah there is nothing to be afraid of, it is like you are arguing with her. If I told you now that worrying about Hannah was silly, you would insist that there is, indeed, a problem and you would still worry." Halscheid advised, "Just reflect when Hannah voices her concerns." Remember, reflecting is when someone repeats what one perceives another person says and feels. So in this case when Hannah expresses that she doesn't want to go to school because she is afraid, Jane should simply reflect by saying something like, "I hear that you're afraid."

In reality, this was exactly what Jane said when she tucked Hannah in bed that night. Hannah settled down immediately while Jane scratched and rubbed Hannah's back. And in the dark my friend's jaw dropped down to her feet in amazement that reflecting worked!

Furthermore, Jane tried to empower her little girl and explained that she could always go to the guidance counselor or nurse in school if she got upset or her tummy hurt. Hannah came home one day happy as a lark as she explained, "My tummy hurt today and I went to the nurse and she helped me. She changed the subject from my tummy hurting and that helped me." So Jane used what her daughter revealed as another springboard. Now Jane was armed with the skills of *reflecting* and *changing the subject*. The next morning Jane started walking Hannah to the bus stop when Hannah confided that her tummy hurt. Jane reflected and then changed the subject, "I hear that your tummy hurts. Ya know, it rained last night." To which Hannah exclaimed, "Ya know, we needed the rain!" Jane laughed at the adult-like words her daughter spoke. Again, my friend was reassuringly surprised that this worked. This reflecting seemed to be a gift to her daughter to help her process and in effect dissipate the problem. On the hotline, I relay this story and simply enlighten parents with the notion that we don't have to have all the answers if we can instead reflect in response to our children's conflicted emotions.

12
INFORMATION IS POWER

Many times on the hotline, parents call about the problem regarding their child not wanting to go to school. Some children seem to be depressed while others seem to be weary or afraid of going to school. Maybe the teacher or classmates are simply not a good fit for your child. Of course, children are notorious for not being able to say what the problem is. It is not that they are being obtuse or difficult on purpose. They really don't know what is bothering them, how to label their feelings or how to articulate their feelings.

Obviously, if a child ever demonstrates any sort of depression or suicidal tendency, a counselor should be consulted. No suicide threat or mental instability should ever be taken lightly. Any cry for help should be taken seriously and attended to professionally.

Also, if bullying is an issue, I would encourage you to involve the school. Of course, you have to be delicate. Guidance counselors and teachers are only human. Perhaps you do not need to volunteer too much information about your child in order not to prejudice anyone. I have often suggested a parent ask a guidance counselor, who could be trusted to be quiet and discreet, to get involved. Perhaps the guidance counselor could sit in the back of a classroom quietly and inconspicuously so the class behaves normally to see and hear if kids get bullied. Also, a good guidance counselor can coach children about socialization skills like how to join in a game on the playground. They can teach the kids not to bully and how to cope with bullying.

The third scenario is that maybe this class or school is just not a good fit for this child. Besides private schools, online schools and home schooling, there are vocational schools which are part of the public school system and don't cost extra money. When I was a child, the vocational school was for the kids who were not academic and were trying to acquire a trade while getting through high school. However, this is no longer the case. So many people are not aware of the extraordinary curriculums the vocational schools offer presently.

I have a friend named Charlene who has twin girls. They had just started eighth grade in the middle school when they came to the realization they didn't like the public high school. One twin, named Rachael, was socially adequate, but still wasn't fond of the school. Her twin, Jessica, was somewhat awkward and had some habits that ended up attracting unwanted and negative attention. Unfortunately, children can be so cruel. According to the story, Jessica hummed when she ate lunch and the kids teased her. Kids seem to be so nasty at this age, anyway. Rachael suggested that her twin sister stop humming, but their mother Charlene was protective and didn't want her child to have to alter her behaviors to conform to these immature and mean girls' expectations. So in the end both girls decided to attend different schools. Rachael chose to go to the local Catholic school, while Jessica went to the vocational school. Now, what you don't know is that their father was a chemical engineer and their mother was both a chemical engineer and a lawyer. Obviously, education was very important to them. I was very surprised and a bit worried about Jessica picking the vocational school. However, to my surprise again, the vocational school was a perfect fit for Jessica. It had a concentrated program in theatre in which she thrived. Jessica was immersed in theatre class for hours every day and formed close-knit friendships due to their common interests, as well as her work ethic, personality and talent. Furthermore, the twin who attended vocational school reportedly often had more academic homework than the twin who went to Catholic school, which was known for its academics and high standards. They have both graduated and gone on to college where they both flourish and I couldn't be more proud or more surprised about their road.

Information is power! You need to find out what is offered in your schools and in your community so you can make educated choices.

13
I NEED YOU TO BE SAFE

Parents seem so quick to say no or yell because they feel put upon or trapped by their kids' needs and requests. It is important to stay on your road of sensibilities. In order to do this, one needs time to think of that road and about the situation at hand. For instance, having time to think about the sleepover your daughter just begged you about may be the difference between exploding or answering calmly and clearly. That is you can say, "I need to think about it." Or "Give me ten minutes by myself to think. If you insist on an answer now it would be no." Giving yourself time allows you to find your bearings and consider that *the most important thing is that my daughter is safe*. So now you can get your ducks in a row and set forth your expectations. The logical expectation is that there has to be a vigilant adult who will be looking in on the sleepover every 10 or 15 minutes.

Years ago my friend, Beth, was watching TV with her daughter, ten at the time. The guest star, Dr. Phil, was on the *Oprah* show and said, "Don't put a child in a situation they are not capable of making decisions about yet." (Beth knew that physically the entire brain doesn't kick in and start working completely until one's twenties.) She said that this made sense and a light bulb went off in her head. Beth and her daughter, Julia, looked at each other, smiled, nodded their heads and realized this was a reasonable baseline for future events. Indeed, this became a theme in their household, so that Beth could always elicit Julia's and her brother's cooperation in keeping them safe in the future. So for instance, when Julia wanted to go to a party or sleepover, Beth would make sure she talked to the parent at the home of the gathering to explain her expectations of what being vigilant meant to her. It turns out that every parent was cooperative, on board and eager to please Beth. Furthermore, the nicest part was Julia never was nasty or resentful of her mother's vigilance. Instead, Julia seemed to be happy her mother went out of her way to look out for Julia's welfare. Julia knew her mother loved her and just needed her to be safe. Beth was clear with her children that she wanted them to have the best life they could and the most fun they could. Beth would offer, "I will take you anywhere you need to go. I will drive you and pick you up. I can give your friends a ride. I will do whatever I can to help you have all the fun you can. I just need you to be safe." *You can't hurt yourself or others* was her mantra.

And true to her word, Beth eagerly chauffeured her children and their friends all the time. This was her job as a parent. Why have children if you treat them as an inconvenience?

I remember many times when Beth drove her daughter and her friends to the roller skating rink on Saturday night. She was aghast to see there were hundreds of kids to only a few staff skating on the rink or working the food stand. Who was watching the kids? Beth could never leave her daughter without supervision, so she stayed even though the loud, blaring, boom-boom of the music tortured her. Sometimes she even left to go sit in the quiet of her car for a few minutes. Beth sat many nights in the skating rink reading a book despite the painfully loud music to ensure her ducklings were properly protected. Julia appreciated her mom sitting at the table with all of their coats. Years later Julia remembered how her mother had gone out of her way for Julia and told her mother how much this meant to her. My friend, Beth, was overwhelmed with the warm fuzzy feeling of accomplishment. Beth felt appreciated for the job of parenting well done.

14

I'M ON YOUR SIDE; FOLLOW THROUGH

I talk on the hotline often about *telling your child you are on their side and then follow through*. You explain, "I want you to have fun. I will drive you and your friends." Make sure when your child needs you to chauffeur them and their friends, you willingly do so with a smile on your face and not a chip on your shoulder. Instead of *you owe me because I'm going out of my way to drive you,* how about imparting the attitude of *I love you and I am proud of myself for going out of my way to help my kid.*

The same thing goes for what your child commits to do for you as the result of you eliciting their cooperation. If your child says he will help set and clear the table, you have to remember to remind him of what he has to do. Be careful of your attitude and *follow through*. As dinner is wrapping up and before anyone gets up, remind everyone about their part in clearing the table. Being consistent and following through is very effective. If you are not vigilant in following through with your agreed upon behaviors, it is unlikely your child will respect them. This is like a law that is never enforced. It's hard to imagine speed limits effective without highway patrolmen enforcing them.

On the other hand, isn't it nice when an officer gives you a warning instead of a ticket? There is a fine line we walk as parents in being consistent and following through with consequences versus being flexible and understanding. Moreover, being flexible and understanding does not exclude you from following through.

So what happens, for instance, when your daughter doesn't adhere to the agreement of *every Friday night her room is clean before she goes out*? You may need to be careful to consider what you say about the limits in your home like, "You can't go out if your room isn't clean." Perhaps, the room being clean isn't so important to the child on a Friday night as the Friday Night Social at school. Even if cleaning her room was the agreement, be careful of the line you draw in the sand. Your child may rebel if pushed into a corner.

Furthermore, the more you show empathy, the more your child may learn empathy. Empathy is when someone can feel what it is like from your point of view. Giving choices is probably a wiser tactic. For instance, "Since you have a party to go to, you have a choice to straighten up before you go or tomorrow morning." Again, you elicit the commitment from your child. But your child still has to toe the line and do what she promised. In this way, you are not backing yourself into a corner to argue with your daughter or lose face the night of a party when emotions are running high. Remember, pick your battles. If you feel your child is pushing you, maybe you started the battle. Following through is important, but so is being flexible. The next morning, perhaps, you and your daughter can work on *not waiting until the last minute to clean her room.*

On a sneaky side note, perhaps if you can clean with your child and you can do so with a positive attitude, you might just be surprised at how your child responds. This is an opportunity to talk with your child. I guarantee there will be plenty of conversation starters while sorting through the rubble. Doing chores together forces you to communicate and cooperate. At the very least, you'll have to ask where they put this or that and "Is this trash?" You may be surprised as you find yearbooks, trophies, games, trash or whatever else makes up your child's room and life, that there's a lot to talk about. If your child agrees to this coupled with your upbeat and positive attitude, it's a great opportunity to have a positive experience accomplishing something together with your child. This becomes another instance where you get your needs of a cleaner room and personal time with your child met.

The point here is that following through time and time again is an integral part of the parenting process, which when coupled with empathy may serve you well.

15
RIPPLE EFFECT

Every action you commit is like throwing a pebble into a pond. When you throw a pebble into a pond, there is a ripple effect. Every action has a consequence.

I can't tell you how many parents call complaining in desperation that their teenage child is volatile in their home. Some kids curse, hit or destroy property. The bottom line is that you are entitled to be safe in your home. When I've asked why the police weren't called in response to their kids acting out, so many parents reveal meekly that they don't want to get their child in trouble. If a stranger was living in your home and destroyed your property or hit you, you would call the police. Why tolerate something less for yourself in relation to your children?

So many parents seem to operate from a guilt perspective. Guilt is defined as feeling that you committed a crime or offense against someone. Get rid of this guilt! You can feel bad that your child is in jail or trouble, but don't take their consequence away from them, because consequences teach right from wrong. If your three-year-old ran into the street, you wouldn't hesitate to stop him. Perhaps, a *time-out* would be a consequence of not following the rule of *not running into the street*. The point here is that you should be clear that the time-out or consequence is imperative so your precious child learns right from wrong, and doesn't run out into the street and doesn't get hit by a car.

Instead of guilt motivating you, your parenting values and skills will motivate you. A good parent is a good teacher and a good manager. A good manger elicits cooperation while a good teacher teaches right from wrong, proper behavior in one's home, and consequences for one's behaviors. Hopefully if a parent is following through from when little William is small, then little William knows "I do get consequences for my actions." Then he will know "I will have to go sit on the *bad boy chair* if I don't follow the rules." Little Andrea would know from experience that "I will have to leave Nana's house for a *time-out* if I have a tantrum." In their teens, both William and Andrea will know that mom and dad are fair and flexible, but there are consequences for their behaviors.

If my children ever hurt me, cursed at me, or purposefully damaged our property, then they would have to make restitution. Remember, *it's not the size of the dog in the fight; it's the size of the fight in the dog.* As loving and supportive to my children as I am, they also know I would not allow anyone to abuse me – not even my children. If you are not clear about your actions, then you will end up throwing the wrong rock into the pond resulting in an undesirable ripple effect.

Another example of a ripple effect is when parents get their feelings hurt by their children. I cringe when I hear a parent bringing up, for example, "I paid for them so you should share your french fries with me!" Is the monetary value of the french fries of the utmost importance here? No, empathy is what you are trying to teach in this moment. You want your child to feel what he would feel like if he were watching and wanting your fries. Here is where you want your child to show empathy, so teach empathy. One can explain, "I feel hurt when you don't share with me. I would share with you." This statement doesn't lord money over one's head as the be-all-end-all. It imparts the notion of *walk in my shoes and see how I feel,* which imparts empathy. The bottom line is look at your own actions as an adult and parent and be cognizant that these actions have consequences. And remember, all anybody can do is *place one foot in front of the other* in finding your road to how you can parent effectively.

16
PORTRAY YOUR FAMILY VALUES

Many parents worry about what's happening outside of their homes. We worry that our six-year-olds are privy to kids cursing on the school bus, for instance. How can we protect our children and make sure they learn right from wrong in the face of negative exterior forces? The truth is you can't control every situation your child is in or what words your child hears on the school bus or the playground. But you can set up expectations for behaviors in your home and around the family. You can portray your family values!

Talking about the cursing issue, a friend went so far as to look up words and their synonyms. This friend asked her kids which synonyms rang a bell and which words would express themselves effectively. Moreover, she elicited their cooperation to commit to using appropriate vocabulary instead of curse words. Then she placed the lists of words on the refrigerator. Although they all agreed, her kids made fun a bit like accentuating a word with sarcasm. But in the end it worked and they all learned new words. This mother got what she needed and her kids were actually learning to use new vocabulary which helped them express themselves better. The kids became a bit more articulate and my friend felt successful! This made her feel like a good mother.

Someone on the hotline called with a similar problem but with an added twist. This nice lady was distraught over her ex-husband's cursing and their children's obvious exposure to this behavior. Of course, authorities could get involved if language became abusive, but I wanted to empower this concerned and nice lady. So I remembered my friend and explained the notion of portraying your family values. Children are extremely adaptable and you can elicit the cooperation and commitment from the kids to follow the house rules. In this case, it was a commitment to choose words other than curse words to express themselves. Because these kids were younger, they would be more likely to see this new rule as a fun and exciting game. Of course, be sure to compliment their good behavior and expressive word choices, especially when they are upset or excited about something. Remember, following through is perhaps the most important skill of parenting.

17
GENERAL CONTRACTOR

A parent is the general contractor of his or her child's life. Just as a general contractor orchestrates a construction project, a parent needs to advocate for his or her child. A child cannot change his situation in school, for instance, and consequently is trapped in an undesirable circumstance. I often speak on the hotline about my friend Amy and her son, Jonathon, because it illuminates how much a child needs our help.

This story takes place when Jonathon was about nine years old and in fifth grade. Jonathon was a good little boy. He was usually well-behaved, quiet and smart. Although his teacher was good at actually teaching class, he had personality traits that Jonathon found to be sarcastic and their personalities did not fit well together. Jonathon became irritated. The teacher, whom we will call Mr. X, could be obnoxious. For example, Amy was sitting in class during a *Back to School Day* when Mr. X was teaching. He was teaching with a lot of energy when two little girls came to the classroom bearing cupcakes for the teachers from one of their birthday celebrations. To Amy's shock, Mr. X licked his fingers and then touched all the cupcakes, so the girls had to leave them all with him! When relaying this story to me, Amy said that I should have seen the little girls' shocked faces!

Over the year, Jonathon became a bit agitated in class, culminating in his punching the wall during gym class and breaking a bone in his hand. Jonathon insisted he was annoyed about other things, but it made Amy wonder what really provoked him to get so angry that he broke his hand. Amy called the guidance counselor who revealed that children can feel stressed when stuck in a situation they cannot do anything about. Jonathon had begun to feel frustrated in his classroom with his teacher. Typically Amy wanted her son to *rise to the occasion* when he felt frustrated with other people. She believed that through life we are forced to deal with all kinds of people, such as neighbors, fellow employees, bosses or committee members. She felt badly that she had not taken into consideration that one difference between children and adults is that adults can change their situations, but children cannot easily make changes for themselves. Jonathon was practically a sitting duck in a classroom with a teacher who was a bad fit for him. How unfortunate that it was already the end of the school year when everything came to a head. But Amy learned her lesson to empower her children and to advocate for her kids in the future. After all, a general contractor orchestrates all of the other contractors working on a building site to make sure things run smoothly.

18

KEEP YOUR EYE ON THE BALL

A football player concentrates only on getting that football down the field to the goalposts and across the goal line. He doesn't worry about the man selling hotdogs in the stands. He has to *keep his eye on the ball*. For instance, so many parents call the hotline about their children in Special Education not getting adequate services in the school. Be careful of your road. So often the gut reaction is to fight with the school to get resources for your child. I believe whole-heartedly in advocating on behalf of your child and trying to get the teachers and child study team to accommodate your child's needs. However, there is a line between advocating and fighting a losing battle. While you fight with the school to tutor your child, your child is floundering. Choose where you expend your energy. Life is a juggling act; so while eliciting cooperation from the school, also find other solutions. Attack the problem from all sides as you keep your eye focused on fixing the problem.

My friend, Penelope, went through the public school system and special education system as did her daughter. However, Penelope's parents hired an amazing special education teacher to tutor her privately. In turn, Penelope made sure her daughter had private tutoring, which in the first few months raised her reading ability by two levels. Penelope believes both she and her daughter would have suffered dramatically if they had not had private teachers. She believes you cannot rely on the public school system for everything all the time. She is so appreciative that her wonderful proactive parents addressed her learning disabilities head on.

The idea of tutoring has been a springboard for her to find help for herself. For instance, because she's dyslexic, she is particularly careful to use spell-check and dictionaries consistently.

Furthermore, Penelope completely disagreed with using an outline in order to write a paper as most teachers instruct. Years ago through someone in a dyslexia organization, she found her own way – *the only way for her to write!* She found and taught herself to use the *Index Card Method.* The Index Card Method uses index cards to write a paper which, through its process, provides clearer organization of one's thoughts.

The Index Card Method is when after research is completed and the text is highlighted, one sentence or one quote is written on each index card. Then after cards are completed, they can be sorted into piles according to subcategories. For instance, if you were doing a written assignment about cars, information about the tires might be sorted into one pile while the paint colors are placed in another pile. As one reads and sorts and rereads the cards, one starts to make sense of it all while continuing to add transition words and their own thoughts and sentences to more cards. A lot of editing and time is essential in this process, but it works! Furthermore, after many attempts at editing, Penelope asks other people to proofread what she's written.

This detailed account of my friend's solutions to compensate for her learning disabilities is to paint a picture of the road she followed over time to address her problem. Advocating for what she needs doesn't end here.

In other areas of her life, Penelope empowers herself to address whatever problems may be at hand. She has learned to sew and enjoys altering the clothing she buys. She doesn't just accept the fit of her clothing to be dictated to her off the rack.

The point here is whether you hire a tutor, switch schools, adopt a different learning style, attend family counseling, or rely on medications that help in managing a disorder, ask yourself, "Are you addressing the issue at hand? Is all of this solving the problem or at least making it better?" Remember, *keep your eye on the ball.*

19
SPRINGBOARD

I want people to find jumping off points or incentives – a springboard to figure out what you feel comfortable doing and what works. You may hear an idea or plan that other parents or professionals incorporate into their own child rearing strategies and you can adapt them to suit you. If someone declares that they have the best solution to x, y or z about your child, you listen, understand the skills presented, and then you can choose to alter them to fit your personality. Describing the concept of an allowance I hope will illuminate my springboard effect.

Many parents are so surprised when their children don't respond favorably to money as a reward. The misconception is that they should be happy to work for money and that money is the be-all-end-all to get any child to jump to do what we want. Then, if they don't react positively to getting rewarded with money, they must be the spawn of the devil! You see, giving allowance is not like the days of old like on the *Andy Griffith Show* when Opie got a quarter for emptying the trash cans in his father's office.

Allowance is for children to learn how to manage their money.

I attended a parenting class and heard a married couple describe how they gave an allowance to their children very systematically. Each child had three boxes. One was for saving. One was for charity. And the third box was for spending. My jaw dropped down to my feet. I knew I could never be that organized. So instead of using this exact system, I used this as a springboard to an idea about allowance and money management. I knew I wouldn't do what these parents did but, I could imagine giving a young child a dollar to spend in a dollar store once per week, for instance.

Of course the house rules would apply; first, you can't hurt yourself or others. So something dangerous like a knife or a toy with small parts would not be allowed. Another example is if the child wants candy, then again the house rules apply – like a certain amount of dessert after lunch which may be a fourth to a half of a sandwich and two carrots, for instance. I use this example because a child's tummy is supposedly only as big as their fist. If you set up the rule to finish a whole sandwich, this may be setting them up for overeating and arguing over mealtime. Remember, know your road and set yourself up for success. So ask doctors and other parents and watch what other normal children eat. Develop a reasonable expectation for mealtime.

Anyway, my springboard allowance philosophy continues with the belief that whatever my child picks at the dollar store should be a happy occasion. I thought I should not belittle or shame the child's choice. I wouldn't want to be shamed for buying a lipstick. We should, in fact, be happy for our child's choice and ask enthusiastically, "Are you happy with what you picked?" After buying the toy, ask with a smile, "Are you happy with your purchase?"

The point of this detailed example is to illuminate how you need to know your road. You can see how from the allowance rules of the two parents in a parenting class, I springboarded to a whole set of allowance scenarios and even food guidelines that could work for me and change as my children grow. My premise or springboard is that *allowance is for children to learn how to manage their money.* My job as a parent is to teach my children how to live.

Furthermore, *there are certain chores we all have to do regardless of whether we get paid to do them or not.* We do chores like brushing our teeth or showering and washing our hair because we need to maintain our health. After all, we don't like it when people in our home smell bad. We live in a society called home and there are certain hygiene expectations. We must portray these values to our children. In other words, from these premises we have to elicit our children's cooperation. Then we must figure out how to motivate them to conduct behavioral change, but money may not motivate them.

I always felt children are trapped because they already have the difficult job of school. Furthermore, children have the job of growing and learning how to feel good about themselves and how to navigate their adolescent worlds. Although some children love and react well to earning money, most need to develop their interests and are better suited for team sports, clubs or other extracurricular activities. Let kids be kids. Developing who one is, how to live, and how one feels about themselves is the important job at hand for our children. Often doing chores for intrinsic reasons is much more motivating than money. Intrinsic means the feelings such as pride, accomplishment, and approval that we feel inside naturally after completing the task at hand.

Some kids do enjoy holding down a part-time job. Other kids may respond positively to a list of extra chores like washing the car which would yield extra money. The main point here is that one may react better to and gain more from intrinsic value rather than monetary rewards.

Be clear that what makes sense to you may not be the motivating incentive for your child. You need money for the mortgage and groceries, but our kids don't. Knowing what makes your child tick may help you springboard to a whole set of parameters that help everyone in your home accomplish daily tasks.

20
EXTRACURRICULAR ACTIVITIES

Many women are stay-at-home moms. In my personal experience watching friends and listening to mothers on the hotline, I have found that this staying home business is not what it's cracked up to be. These stay-at-home caretakers are often isolated, lonely and bored. Here's a story of what can happen to a person without extracurricular activities and interests. My friend, Isabel, was such a stay-at-home mom. She would have only her thoughts to accompany her while folding the laundry or doing other mundane chores. Playing with toddlers is noble, but not necessarily stimulating. So when she had a little argument with her husband, he went to work the next day and she was left churning the issue and argument around in her head. She would be wringing her hands over things. That night her husband would return home, surprisingly happy, while she was overwrought about the disagreement they had had the night before. While she was still dwelling on the night before, he said to Isabel, "It's no big deal. People argue. I still love you." The big surprise here was that he hadn't given it any thought because at work he had to attend to the problems at hand. Her husband's mind was stimulated, whereas, Isabel had nothing to keep her mind busy. This is one reason I talk about how extracurricular activities are so good for people. Having hobbies or interests keeps you busy and keeps your brain stimulated, and this makes for a happier you.

In fact, both adults and children who have extra-curricular activities, like belonging to a team sport or club or a routine of going to the fitness center, seem happier and more content. I believe it is incumbent on parents to elicit their children's cooperation to develop their interests. You keep explaining, "I need you to develop your interests." You explain that "It is incumbent upon me to make sure you are devel-oping your interests," or "It is my responsibility to help you learn to develop your interests."

I feel so strongly about having extracurricular interests that I disagree with school administra-tions when they kick a kid off of a team because the child has not kept his or her grades up. I understand schools need to have standards for their academics and thus consequences for not succeeding academi-cally. However, I do not agree with cutting a student loose due to poor grades. The team sport might be the only situation in which this child excels and feels good. So when a child is floundering, another activity may be their only lifeline.

It would be counter-productive if you have a bad day at work and came home and I told you, "Well, you had a bad day so now you can't exercise or watch TV tonight." In fact, exercise might be the only thing that breathes new life into your spirit. Perhaps, after your walk or run and shower you are able to have a good night's sleep and are ready to face the work-place again.

Similarly, teams and clubs may be the lifeline a child has. Instead of kicking a child off the team, maybe the team members could tutor this child. But kicking him or her off a team or club is like throwing a troubled child to the wolves. Furthermore, many parents use their children's extracurricular activities as a consequence. If a child doesn't study or do well on a test or in a class or do a chore, the parent takes the activity away. I believe this is terrible because in the end it is ineffective. Would you take away brushing their teeth or showering or eating break-fast if your child's grade is suffering? I believe your child's chess club or art class or dance class or soccer team are the nutrients for the soul and mind. In the long run, these activities will develop your child's self-esteem long after math class is over.

21
ADDICTIONS

On the hotline I explain that we all have addictions. Addictions are things we habitually do. Addictions are things we may ingest or do or experience to make us feel good, and without them we would feel unhappy and even anxious. That is, we medicate ourselves. We indulge in food, drugs or entertainment to make ourselves feel better.

Most people are familiar with addictions to substances or substance abuse. For instance, alcohol, like other drugs, is a mind altering substance. Alcohol literally impairs your thinking and coordination and alters your mood. Alcohol mars your judgment, kills brain cells, stresses organs and is associated with many illnesses. Furthermore, there are many other kinds of things with which we medicate ourselves.

Believe it or not, food is another good example of how we medicate ourselves. Of course, we need food to survive, but we use it in extraordinary ways. Primarily, whether we are lactose intolerant or have peanut or gluten allergies, diverticulitis, salt reactions or diabetes, we often eat certain foods to appease our finicky systems. Moreover, we all have discerning tastes involving what foods we like and crave, even for instance, preferences for brands of ice cream, chocolate and coffee. That is, not only do we choose foods for nutritional value and medical issues, but we also choose foods because of the fun of the taste of it. We have to eat that piece of chocolate or have our cup of coffee and without it we would be more than unhappy. We probably would even experience anxiety over doing without our habitual treats.

In counseling terms, when we do something to make us feel good, it is called medicating ourselves. We all medicate ourselves. We eat certain foods on a whim to make us feel good, watch TV to entertain ourselves to make us feel good, or exercise to improve our bodies and mood to make us feel good.

Everyone would agree that exercise is very good for you. It is good for you for weight control, muscle tone, mood stabilization and tension release. However, let's be clear that exercise is, indeed, something we do to medicate ourselves. Many of us know a loved one who has to hit that gym or practice to get in shape for that marathon. Although these are commendable efforts, how much time does exercise take up in your life? Furthermore, exercise can cause injuries like muscle and tendon pulls or tears which often lead to physical therapy or surgeries. Although exercise is good for us, exercise can be an addiction and people who exercise routinely would feel anxious if they couldn't exercise.

Another common example of a habitual pastime is watching TV. This can become a problem when, for instance, one's husband watches sports incessantly and the marriage suffers because he's not paying enough attention to his wife and his marriage. Anything with which you medicate yourself that interferes with your relationship carries a red flag of becoming an addiction. I'm not saying don't have addictions. I'm saying be careful of which addictions you allow yourself to indulge.

A wise man, Michael Burk (actually, my husband), once postulated that "Addictions are like snakes. All snakes bite, but some are a lot more dangerous than others." He continued, "So which snake do you pick up; the TV snake or the cocaine snake; the alcohol snake or the exercise snake?" Of course one chooses the TV and exercise snakes!

Consequently, this is why I always encourage people to develop their interests. It is imperative to set up your life surrounded by interests that you enjoy, look forward to, captivate your mind, and make you feel good; so indulge in the healthier, benign addictions and stay away from addictions that have an incredibly high risk.

22

ROUTINE

Routine is essential to a healthy lifestyle. The people I see who are most content have a routine of work and extracurricular activities. Representatives from The National Alliance for the Mentally Ill (NAMI 1-800-950-NAMI or 1-800-950-6264) came to a Crisis Hotline meeting to speak. One of the speakers spoke about how important a routine was for people with mental illness. This struck a chord with me as I thought of my diabetic friend who had a very steady routine. She religiously went to her doctor and took her medicine. She routinely ate certain kinds of food and certain quantities of food. She habitually exercised daily and stretched as often because she exercised so much. And she tried to go to bed at a reasonable time so her sleep cycle remained on a schedule. Remember, *life is a juggling act*. My friend attacked her illness daily from all sides so as to ensure the best results. Her routine seemed to be her method of operation and, ultimately, her strength.

Make no mistake about it. Everyone has something with which to deal. One person has bipolar disorder to manage. Another person has arthritis, while still another has heart disease to handle. Many people struggle with weight issues, while others handle low self-esteem. Everybody has something. Nobody goes unscathed. So find your routine. That's not to say one can't be flexible, but the people who have a routine seem healthier and happier. Fill your life up with such things as a job, volunteering, activities and exercise.

23
I HOPE

In conclusion, my hope is that I have given you hope. My dear, loving father told me when I was a teenager that "there is always hope." "Remember ... hope is a good thing, maybe, hope is the best of things," said Andy Dufresne's character from the movie, *The Shawshank Redemption.*

I hope that you will continue to search for clues that lead you to your road. Adjust your path as is necessary, as new information and ideas come to you and as you find certain strategies to be more or less successful while your family grows and changes. I do not mean to suggest that if you change a behavior, then your life will be perfect because I can assure you that will not happen. But, hopefully, you will find some peace of mind when you stumble upon what behaviors work better.

I hope you find some shining and satisfying moments. Of course, there are many extenuating circumstances in one's family. For instance, like I recently heard on the hotline, a woman's nineteen-year-old son was both bipolar and had substance abuse issues. The mother on the hotline was clear that she could not change her sick son unless he wanted to change and that she needed her home to be safe in the meantime. She couldn't have this sick young man physically hurting others in their home nor could she tolerate him stealing things to sell for drug money. Her hope was to at least find peace in her home, being safe and being there when her son *hit bottom* to help him find the support he needed. It broke her heart as well as her other children's hearts, but her road was going to be eliciting the commitment of her family to not let him in their house. Her hope, short term, was to find peace and safety in her home.

I hope that you feel solace in the fact that you're not alone. All parents struggle with, "What does it mean to be a parent?" and "How do I get my kids to be polite, clean their rooms and do their homework?" and "What can I do now, so that my children are functioning and happy adults later?"

I hope you can learn to see a more positive perspective in a situation and in your children's behaviors. People call the hotline in despair and after I propose a different perspective, they seem to feel better. Maybe their feeling better was because another human being they reached out to listened and empathized. However, I have always had a feeling that the new perspective offered was the key to their renewed and uplifted attitude. Often I have even said in response to their change of mood, "I haven't changed the problem. The same problem exists. But now you see it differently and can move forward to change your behavior." The more positive the perspective, the happier you will feel or at least the less despair you will experience. Therefore, with both labeling in a positive light and working on our behaviors, the more energy and hope we will have to try different solutions and move forward.

I hope that you find your niche in life while encouraging your children to develop their interests. Of course, it is wonderful to have family and friends who love and support us and spend time with us. Moreover, I believe what makes us happy or content in life is our work and extracurricular activities. Having purpose and an avenue to expend our physical, mental and creative energies is what truly makes us feel good.

I hope you continue to look for directions to find your road.

24
MANTRAS

- Find your road.
- A good parent is a good teacher and a good manager.
- *Do more of the same that didn't work to begin with.* (This was a sarcastic quote which, of course, means *don't do more of the same that didn't work to begin with.)*
- Try something different.
- You can't change other people; you can only change yourself.
- What can I do differently?
- Springboard to new ideas, perspectives and parameters.
- Necessity is the mother of invention.
- Just put one foot in front of another.
- Information is power.
- Portray your family values.
- Pick your battles.
- Every situation is a teachable moment.
- Don't be negative and nasty; be positive and pleasant.
- Turn a situation into a positive.
- Don't act like a kid on the playground.

- "Just a spoonful of sugar helps the medicine go down."
- By eliciting others' cooperation, one can get one's own needs met.
- You can't put your head on your child's body.
- Reflecting is listening which is a gift to your children.
- Every one of my behaviors is like throwing a pebble into the pond which causes a ripple effect.
- Teach empathy.
- Keep your eye on the ball.
- Don't expect your child to be perfect or you will be disappointed.
- Don't put a child in a situation they are not capable of making decisions about yet.
- I need you to be safe.
- You can't hurt yourself or others.
- Advocate for your child.
- Empower your child.
- People who seem to be the happiest and most content have a routine of work (or school) and extracurricular activities.
- Life is a juggling act.
- There is always hope.
- Give your children what they need.

WORKS CITED

Fulghum, Robert. *It Was On Fire When I Lay Down On It*. New York: Random House Group, 1989. 14-18. Print.

Kaye. "Thoughts On Failure." B'nai Tikva, Newsletter Shofar (n.d.): n.p. Print.

Made in the USA
Middletown, DE
27 December 2015